Our Inside Story

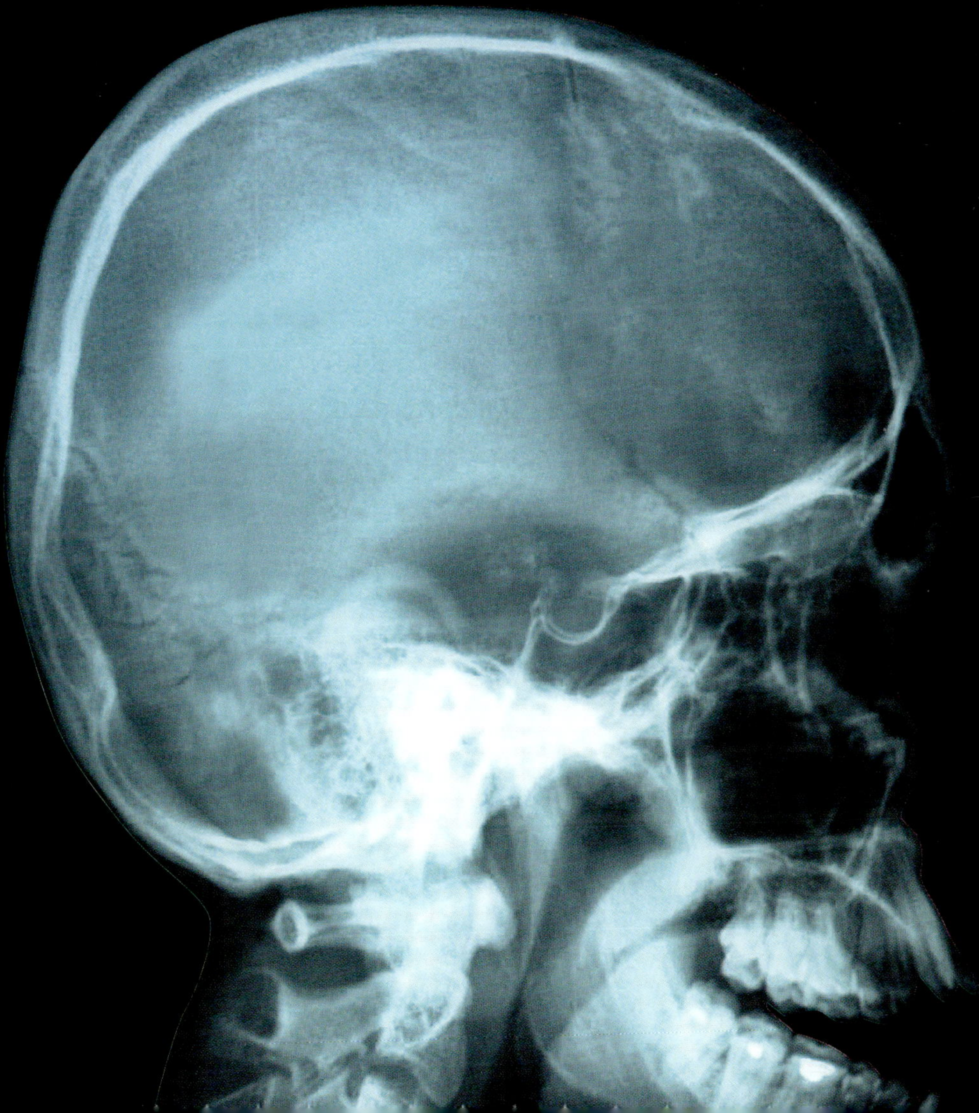

Contents

The Real Story	4
A Closer Look	6
In Your Genes	8
Nature and Nurture	10
Nerve Central	12
All in Your Head	14
Dozing Off	16
Seek and Destroy	18
Go with the Flow	20
Take a Deep Breath	22
Muscle Power	24
Living Bones	26
Spare Parts	28
Glossary	30
Index	31
Research Starters	32

Features

Who was the doctor that prescribed bloodletting, vomiting and singing for his patients? Turn to page 5 to find out.

Genetics and *genealogy* sound similar, but are they? Find out on page 9.

Are people who are good at maths simply born with the ability? Read **Natural Genius?** on page 11 and make up your own mind.

How much of our lives do we spend asleep? Go to page 17 to learn the amazing answer.

Why are sick people often feverish?
Visit **www.infosteps.co.uk**
for more about **ILLNESS**.

The Real Story

People today know far more about how the human body works than ever before. Doctors have tried to treat diseases for thousands of years, but it was not until the 1500s that people really began to understand the human body. Before then it was believed to be wrong to study human **cadavers** so doctors could only study wounds and the bodies of animals.

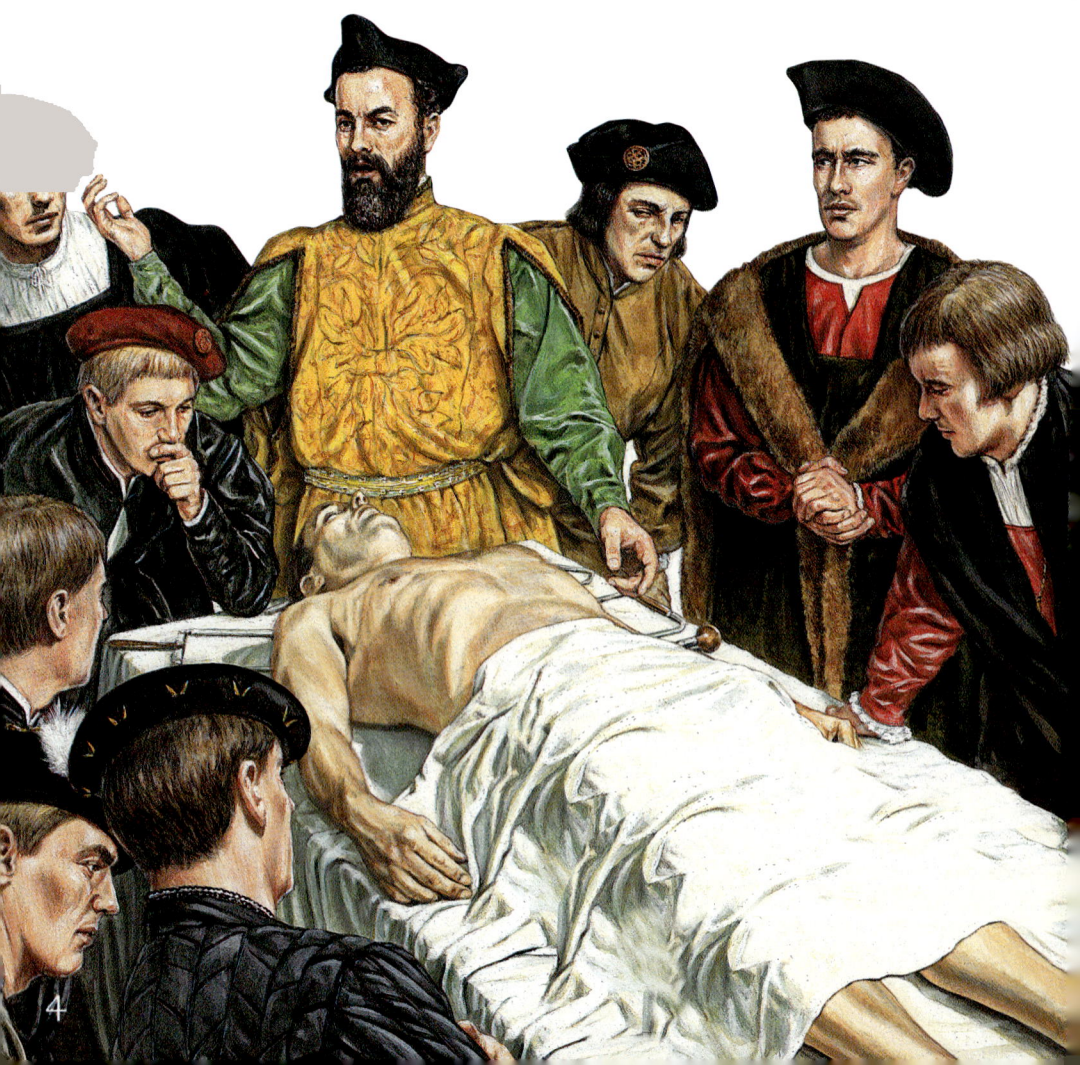

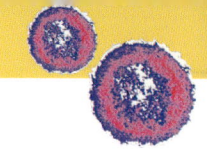

In 1543 the first book containing detailed drawings of human bodies was published. This led to the development of the modern science of **anatomy**. Anatomy looks at the shape and structure of the body and how it is made. The study of how the body works is called **physiology**.

IN FOCUS

Claudius Galen was a famous Roman doctor whose teachings were followed for 1,200 years. Galen believed that the body was made up of four liquids: blood, phlegm, yellow bile and black bile. He thought that illnesses were caused by an imbalance in the liquids. Galen's treatments included bloodletting, vomiting and singing!

It wasn't until the Renaissance period (about 1350–1600) that medical students were allowed to study actual human bodies.

A Closer Look

Over the years our knowledge of both anatomy and physiology has been greatly advanced by new technology.

The microscope, invented about 1608, showed that our bodies are made up of billions of cells. X-rays were discovered in 1895, allowing doctors to see inside the body without cutting it open. In the twentieth century computer technology that scanned the body and produced internal pictures which could be viewed on a screen became available. This technology has made the **diagnosis** and treatment of diseases such as cancer easier.

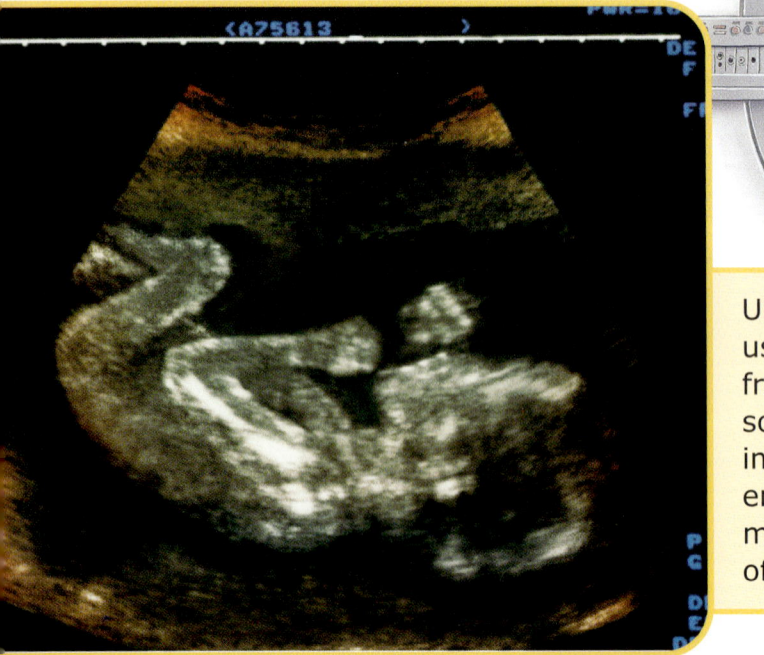

Ultrasound scanners use the echoes from high-pitched sounds to make images. These enable doctors to monitor the health of unborn babies.

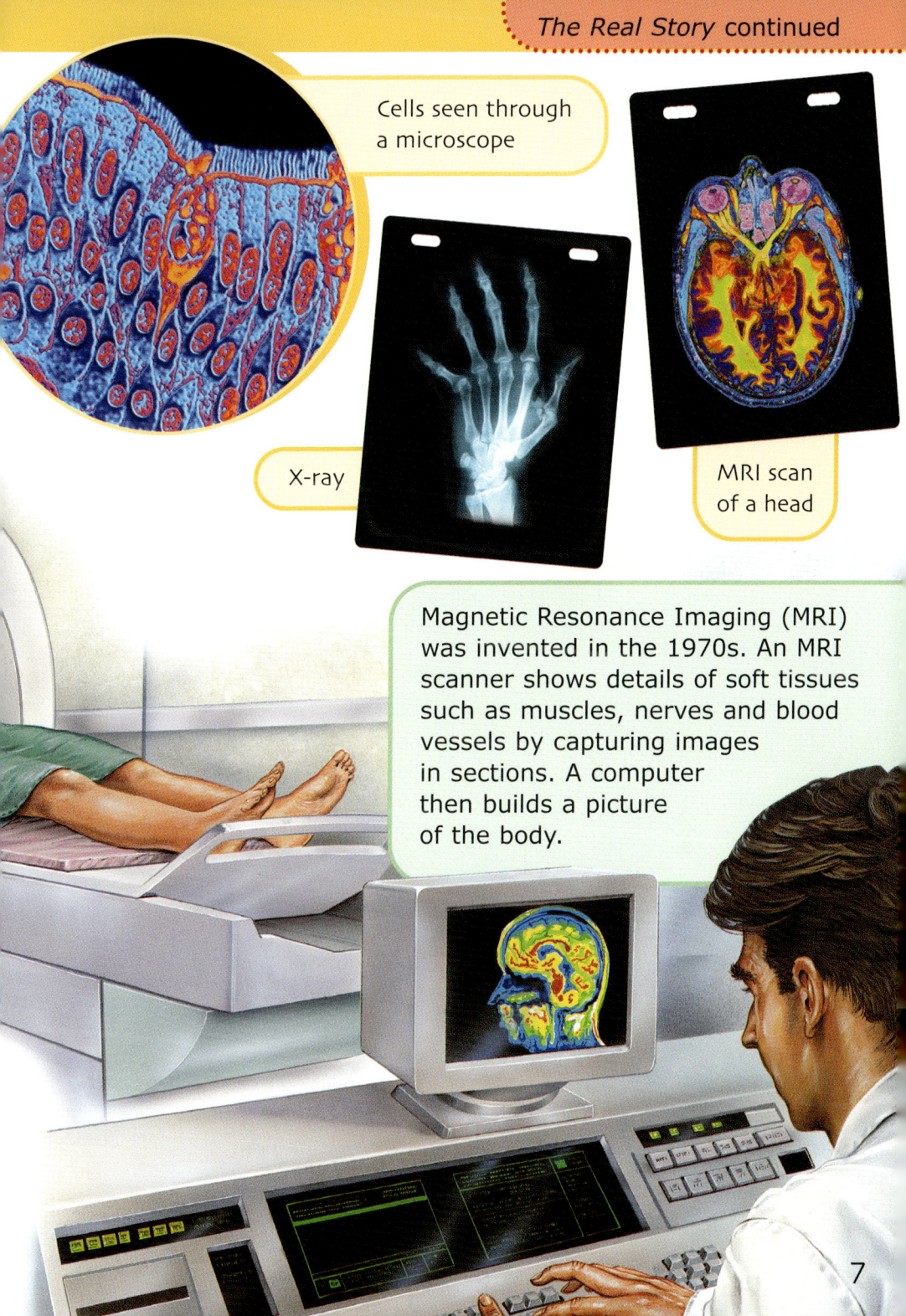

The Real Story continued

Cells seen through a microscope

X-ray

MRI scan of a head

Magnetic Resonance Imaging (MRI) was invented in the 1970s. An MRI scanner shows details of soft tissues such as muscles, nerves and blood vessels by capturing images in sections. A computer then builds a picture of the body.

7

In Your Genes

Why do you look more like your relatives than other people? The answer is in your genes. Genes are the parts of your cells that determine your personal **traits**. We inherit half of our genes from each parent.

When we are born the stages of our growth are already encoded in our genes. Genes direct the growth of cells. They do this thanks to an amazing chemical called DNA. Genes are actually made of DNA. DNA is the short name for deoxyribonucleic acid.

Why do many Scottish people have red hair? About a third of the Scottish population have the "ginger gene", which causes red hair, fair skin and freckles. It is a **recessive** gene which means it won't show up unless it is inherited from both parents. If one parent passes down the black hair gene instead the child will have black hair. That is because black hair is a **dominant** gene.

Genes influence many individual traits such as whether you are male or female and whether you are tall or short. There are at least 30,000 different genes in each human being and scientists still have a lot to discover about how genes work.

DNA is made up of two strands arranged like a long twisted ladder. It contains all the body's genes. DNA forms into threads called chromosomes, shown above.

WORD BUILDER

The scientific study of genes is called genetics not genealogy as you might expect. Genealogy is the study of family origins to create a family tree; it is not a science. People have been studying their family history for a very long time, but scientists didn't know what genes were until the mid-1900s.

Nature and Nurture

Physical traits such as eye colour are determined mostly or entirely by genes so we say they are due to nature. The things that happen to you in your life—your experiences, the people you know, the places you live—add up to what we call nurture.

Hundreds of different traits make up who you are, and most of these develop through a combination of nature and nurture. Your taste for certain foods, for example, is influenced by both.

In Your Genes continued

Natural Genius?

My whole family was never any good at maths so I guess I never will be either. It's just the way I was born so why should I even try?

I think anyone can be good at maths like me if they study hard and have a positive attitude.

IN FOCUS

One way that scientists try to understand nature and nurture is by studying identical twins who have been separated at a young age. Since they were born with exactly the same genes it is thought that differences in personality or physical characteristics will be due to nurture, or growing up in different environments with different influences.

Nerve Central

Our nerves, brain and spinal cord make up our nervous system. Nerves link the brain to every part of the body. They are long and thin—some nerve cells, or **neurons**, are up to 1 metre long! Other neurons are shorter than 0.1 of a centimetre. Nerves work full-time gathering information for the brain about things such as body temperature. Motor neurons then deliver the brain's instructions to the muscles.

How Nerves Work

Spidery dendrites pick up signals. The signals travel along an axon before passing to other nerve cells across tiny gaps called synapses.

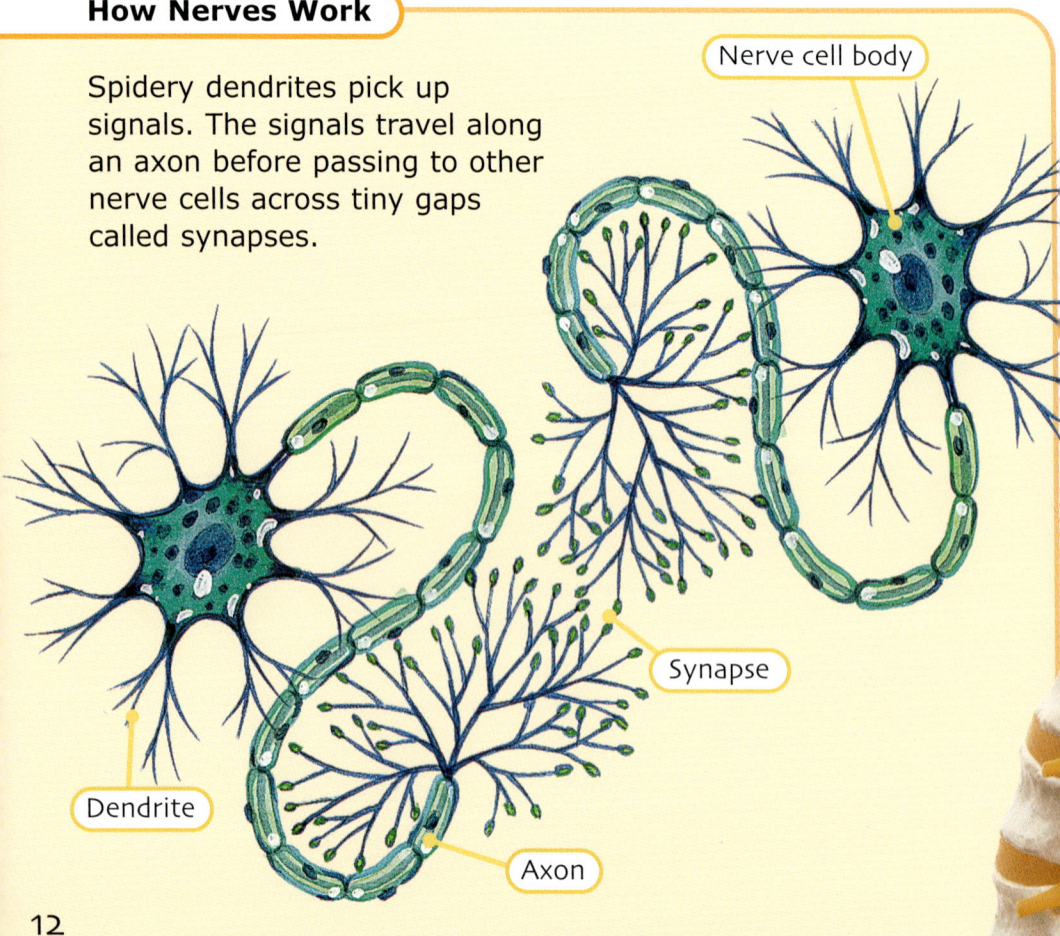

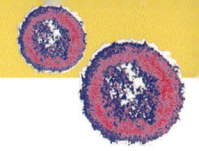

The main nerve is the spinal cord which is a bundle of millions of nerve cells with long fingers. The spinal cord is about 46 centimetres long. Branches of nerves connect it to our skin, muscles and other body parts. One end of the spinal cord joins with the brain while the other becomes a cord inside the vertebrae of the lower back.

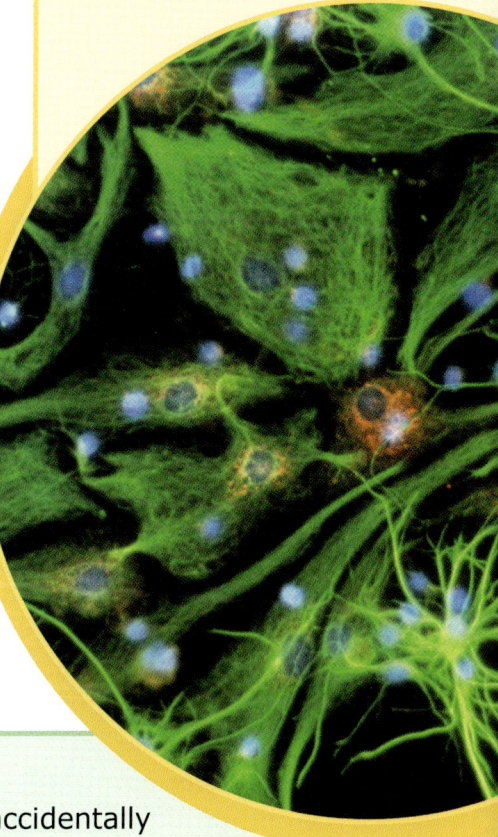

In this magnified image of nerve cells you can easily see the feathery dendrites and the long stringy axons.

OUCH!

If you accidentally burn your fingers your spinal cord instantly sends an urgent message to your arm telling it to pull your hand away. These kinds of quick automatic reactions are called reflexes.

All in Your Head

The brain is our most complex and delicate organ. For many years people believed we used only 10% of our brain in everyday life. Brain scans have now shown that we use all parts of our brain at different times. Even damage to small areas of the brain can cause problems such as memory loss, difficulty with speaking, mood swings and personality changes.

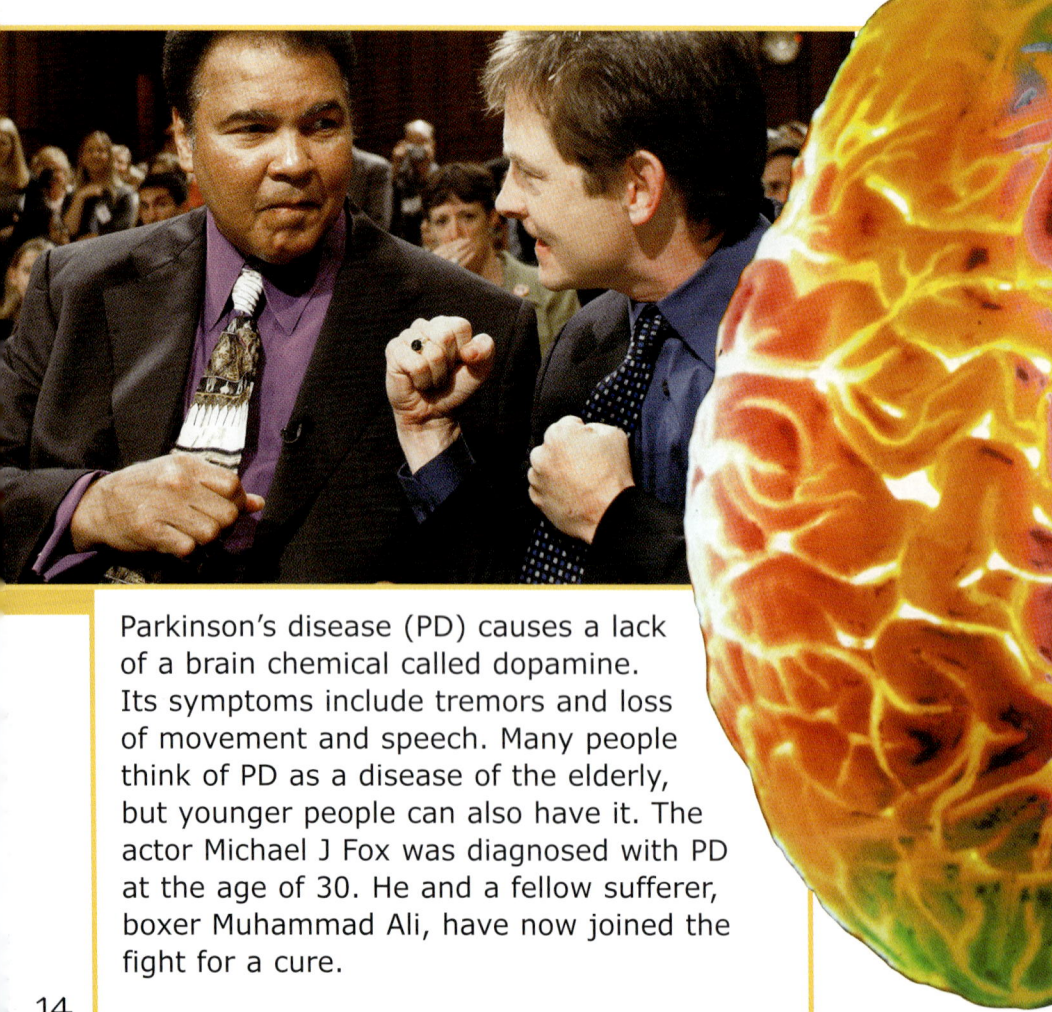

Parkinson's disease (PD) causes a lack of a brain chemical called dopamine. Its symptoms include tremors and loss of movement and speech. Many people think of PD as a disease of the elderly, but younger people can also have it. The actor Michael J Fox was diagnosed with PD at the age of 30. He and a fellow sufferer, boxer Muhammad Ali, have now joined the fight for a cure.

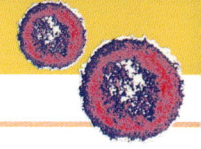

A Brain of Two Halves

Do you know your brain has two halves? The left half controls the right side of your body and the right half controls the left side of your body. Scientists believe the left brain is good with logic and detail while the right brain is better at seeing the "big picture". For example, your left brain would probably read the proverb "curiosity killed the cat" as a warning about pet safety! You need the right side of your brain to understand the wider meaning of the proverb.

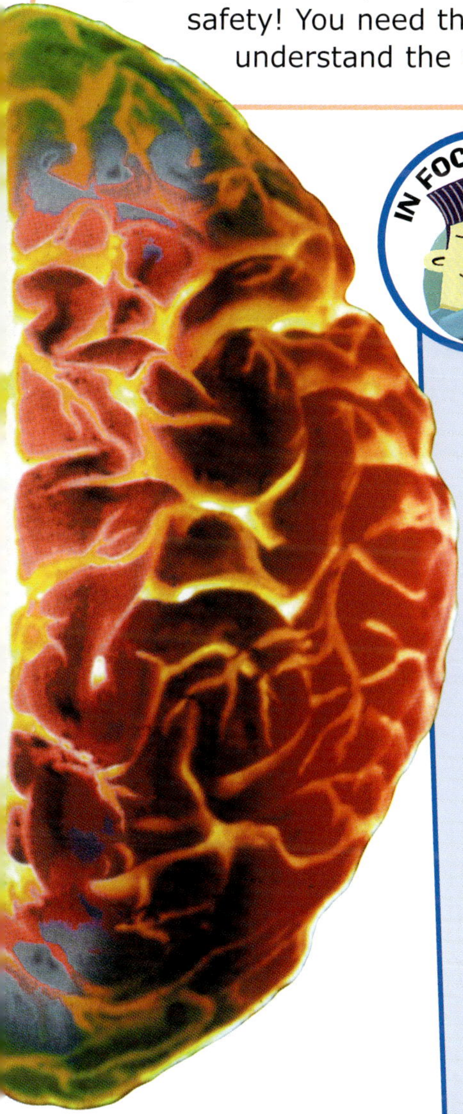

IN FOCUS

About one in ten people is left-handed. The reason why we are left- or right-handed is still a mystery. Below are some famous "lefties". Do you know of more?

- Ludwig van Beethoven (composer)
- Bill Clinton (US president)
- Celine Dion (singer)
- Albert Einstein (physicist)
- Jimi Hendrix (musician)
- Julius Caesar (emperor)
- Pelé (soccer player)
- Keanu Reeves (actor)
- Julia Roberts (actress)
- Bart Simpson (cartoon character)
- Leonardo da Vinci (artist)
- Oprah Winfrey (TV star)

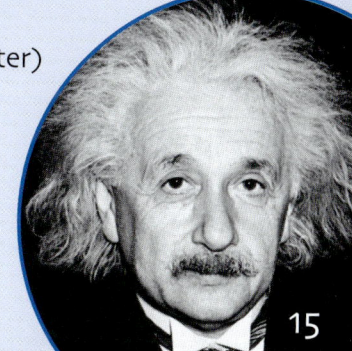

Dozing Off

You can live longer without food than you can without sleep. If you miss one night's sleep you'll be tired and irritable. If you miss two nights you'll have trouble thinking, and doing anything will be difficult. If you go without sleep for five days you will start to **hallucinate** and you may die. Your brain can't maintain vital body functions. Not getting enough sleep can be serious!

Even though the body is resting scientists know that the brain works all night. When you sleep your **conscious** brain switches off and your **subconscious** takes over. Sometimes the two states overlap, however, such as when you daydream or when a dog barking outside enters your dream while you sleep.

Many people talk and even walk while they are asleep. They are not acting out their dreams. Their brains just don't stop giving commands to their muscles.

FAST FACTS

Insomnia, or sleeplessness, affects many people. However, by the age of 60 most people will have spent about 20 years sleeping!

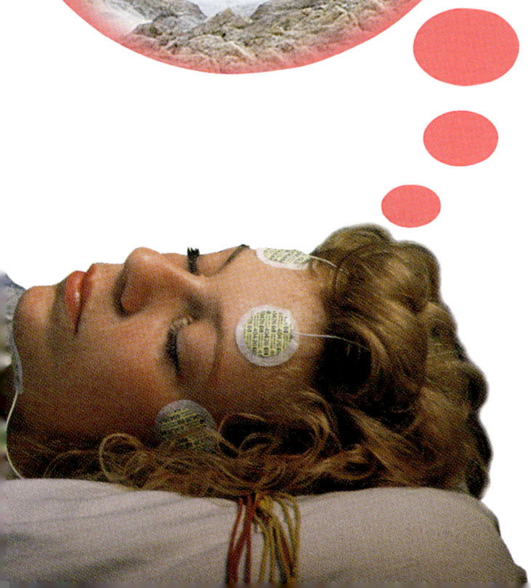

By attaching electrodes to sleeping people and studying their brain activity scientists discovered that there are two different kinds of sleep. One of these is called rapid eye movement (REM) sleep because the eyes flick rapidly back and forth. The other kind of sleep is called non-REM (NREM). Most dreams occur during REM sleep.

Seek and Destroy

Your immune system is a network of cells and organs that defends your body from poisons and germs. It is made up of white blood cells, the chemicals they make and the organs that produce them. Some white blood cells live in your tissues. Others patrol the body through the **circulatory system**, moving where they're needed to repel bacteria, viruses and other invaders.

Sometimes your immune system is *too* ready to attack and it turns on foreign things that are actually harmless, such as pollen, some foods and even the droppings of tiny dust mites. This is how allergies occur.

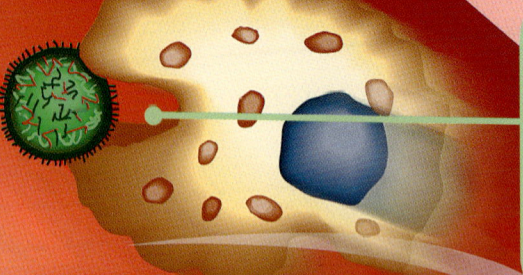

Macrophages are the largest white blood cells. They are our bodies' rubbish collectors, cleaning up wastes and destroying invaders. Here a macrophage is about to swallow a germ.

Why are sick people often feverish?
Visit **www.infosteps.co.uk**
for more about ILLNESS.

Hay fever is an allergy to airborne pollens.

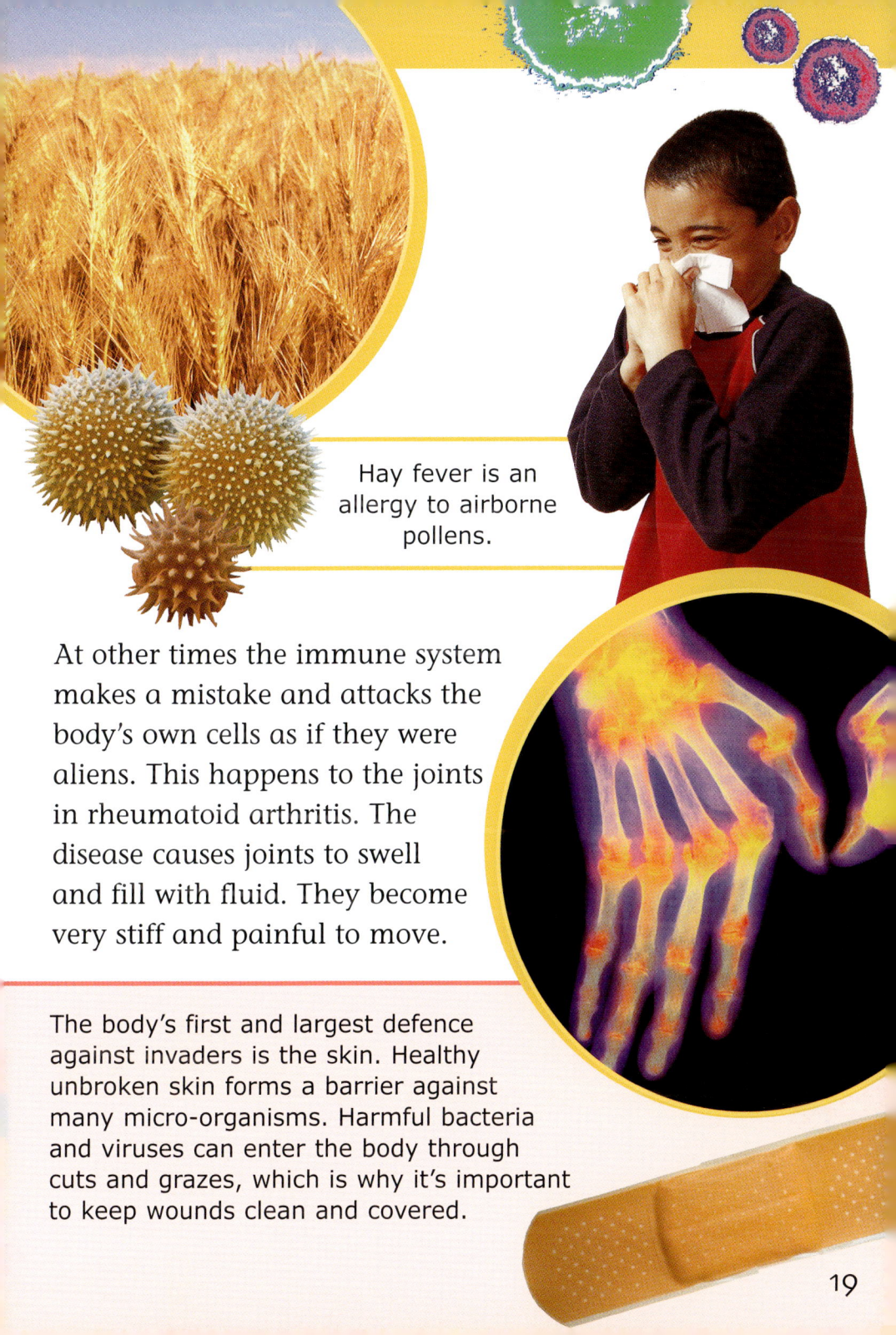

At other times the immune system makes a mistake and attacks the body's own cells as if they were aliens. This happens to the joints in rheumatoid arthritis. The disease causes joints to swell and fill with fluid. They become very stiff and painful to move.

The body's first and largest defence against invaders is the skin. Healthy unbroken skin forms a barrier against many micro-organisms. Harmful bacteria and viruses can enter the body through cuts and grazes, which is why it's important to keep wounds clean and covered.

19

GO WITH THE FLOW

IN FOCUS

You are a red blood cell. Your mission is to carry oxygen to all the cells in your human's body.

START

You are created in the bone marrow.
Throw dice and move.

Millions of red blood cells join you in a single drop of blood.

Your human's heart pumps you around the body.

You stop at the lungs to pick up oxygen.
Your opponent swims ahead one space.

Blood cells float in plasma which contains nutrients and other substances.

You rush along a giant artery.
Throw again.

You turn into a narrow capillary.
Go back two spaces.

Ouch! Your human accidentally cuts herself. It's lucky you weren't squeezed outside.
Flow on one space.

A mosquito nearly has your opponent for lunch
Flow on one space

Uh-oh! Germs enter the wound. White blood cells fight the invaders.
Miss 2 turns.

Tiny particles called **blood platelets** form a blood clot in the wound.
Miss a turn.

The clot over your human's cut dries into a protective scab.

20

Your human donates blood.

Gush ahead two spaces.

In your human's kidneys blood is filtered and excess water is removed.

Surge forward one space.

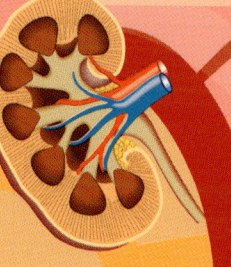

Blood banks test and store blood from blood donors.

The spleen removes dead blood cells and makes new white blood cells.

Emergency! Your human has been hurt and is losing blood quickly.

Go back one space.

Your human has anaemia (too few red blood cells). She feels tired and weak.

Rest for one throw.

Blood makes up one-tenth of the body's weight.

Your human's blood type does not match that of a donor.

Drift back two spaces.

You reach the liver. It collects nutrients and filters poisons from the blood.

As you lose oxygen you start to turn purple.

Time to catch a vein back to the lungs!

After 120 days your time is up. Never mind – bone marrow churns out millions of red blood cells every second!

END

Take a Deep Breath

We can go for days without food or water, but without air our bodies would die within minutes. That's because the oxygen in the air is an essential part of the energy-giving chemical reactions inside each cell. Air enters through the nose and mouth and goes down the windpipe, or trachea, before reaching our lungs. The lungs absorb the oxygen and pass it into the blood which carries it to all body cells.

Carbon dioxide, the body's main waste, passes from the blood to the air in the lungs. From there it goes up the windpipe and out the nose or mouth.

The Tree of Life

Our two lungs are like trees. They each have a hollow main trunk called the bronchus. The bronchus divides into many branches called bronchioles. Each bronchiole leads to a cluster of tiny buds called alveoli. At the alveoli oxygen is taken into the bloodstream and carbon dioxide is passed out.

IN FOCUS

Asthma is a common illness in young people. Sufferers of asthma have difficulty breathing because of swollen air passages. Asthma can be triggered by allergies, sickness or physical activity. It is easily controlled with inhaled medicine.

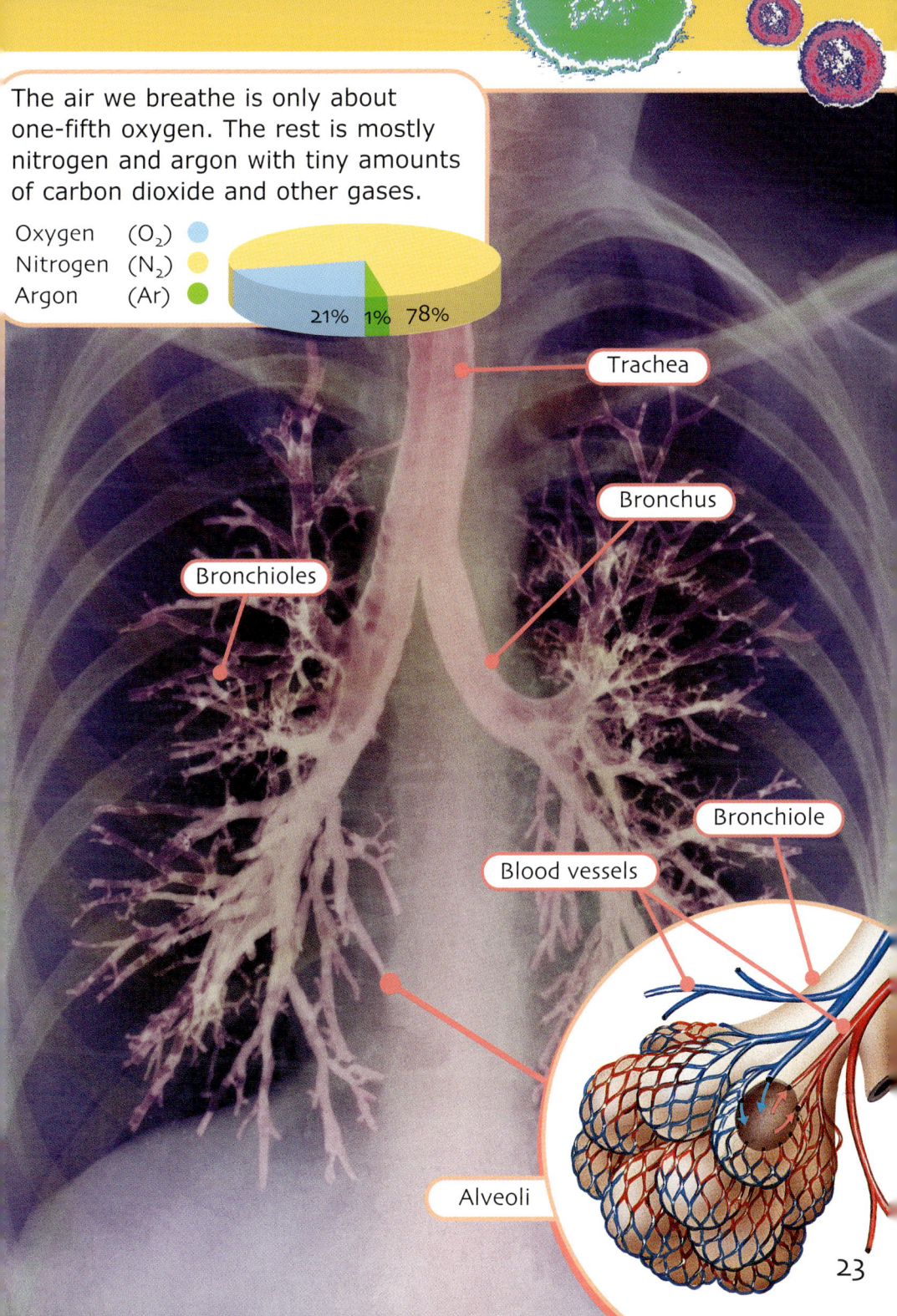

Muscle Power

Muscles allow our bodies to move. They convert energy into pulling power. We can control some of our muscles, but others such as the heart and stomach work without our conscious thought. The ones we can control are called **skeletal** muscles. We have about 650 of them. They attach to our bones with thick ropes of tissue called tendons.

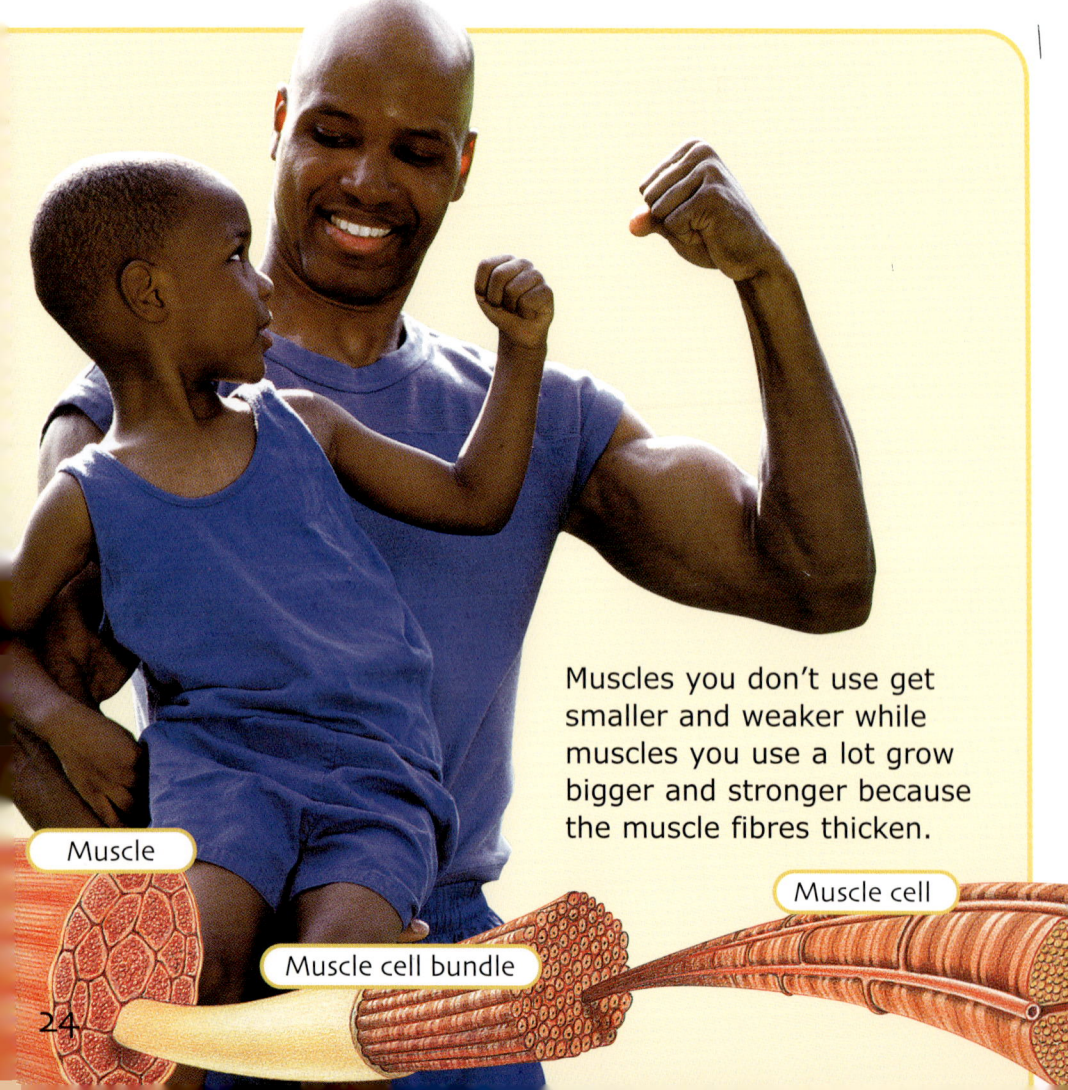

Muscles you don't use get smaller and weaker while muscles you use a lot grow bigger and stronger because the muscle fibres thicken.

Muscle

Muscle cell

Muscle cell bundle

Bundles of muscle cells make up our muscles. Each muscle cell is made up of smaller bundles of fibres called myofibrils. Within each myofibril thin strands of protein surround thick ones. When a muscle contracts the thick strands pull the thin ones closer together. Each cell, and the muscle, shortens.

Many muscles work in pairs. For example, the biceps muscle in your arm pulls the forearm bone to bend the elbow. Its partner, the triceps muscle, pulls the other way to straighten the elbow. Muscles must contract to create movement. That's why it's important to stretch your muscles before and after exercise.

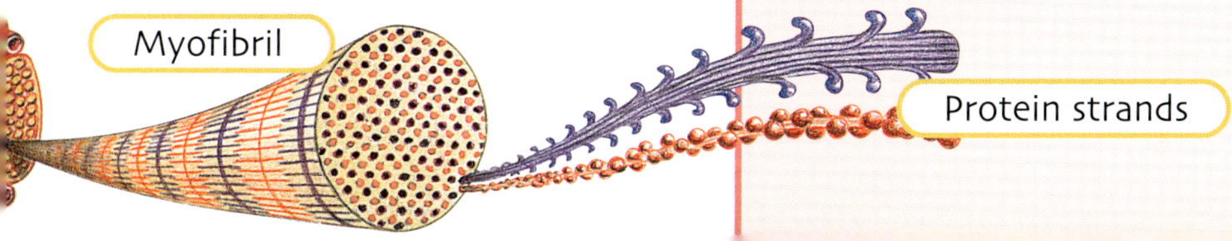

FAST FACTS

Every time you smile you are using about 30 muscles in your face!

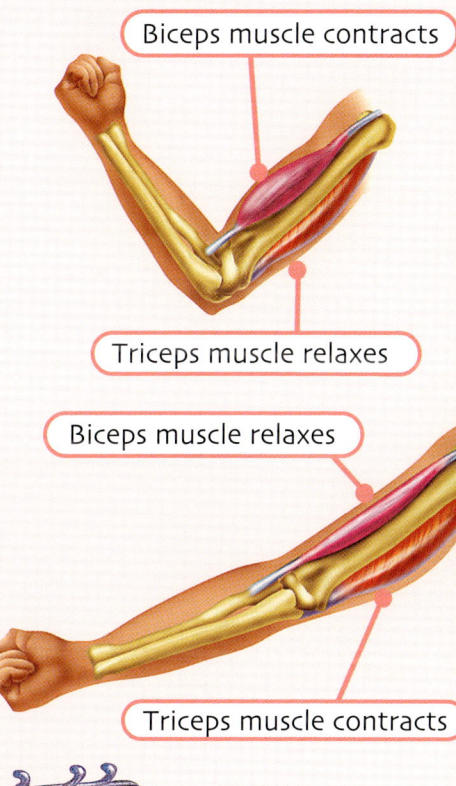

Biceps muscle contracts

Triceps muscle relaxes

Biceps muscle relaxes

Triceps muscle contracts

Myofibril

Protein strands

25

Living Bones

Bone is living tissue. It grows and changes throughout your life. Bone tissue is a mixture of three main substances. One is collagen, which is a mesh of fibres that lets bone bend without snapping. The second substance is crystals, made up of minerals such as calcium that make bones tough and hard. The third substance is millions of cells called osteoblasts, which build and maintain the collagen and mineral crystals.

Like other body parts bones have blood vessels to bring them nutrients and nerves to detect pressure and pain. As you exercise the pull of muscles stimulates new bone growth. Strong muscles make strong bones.

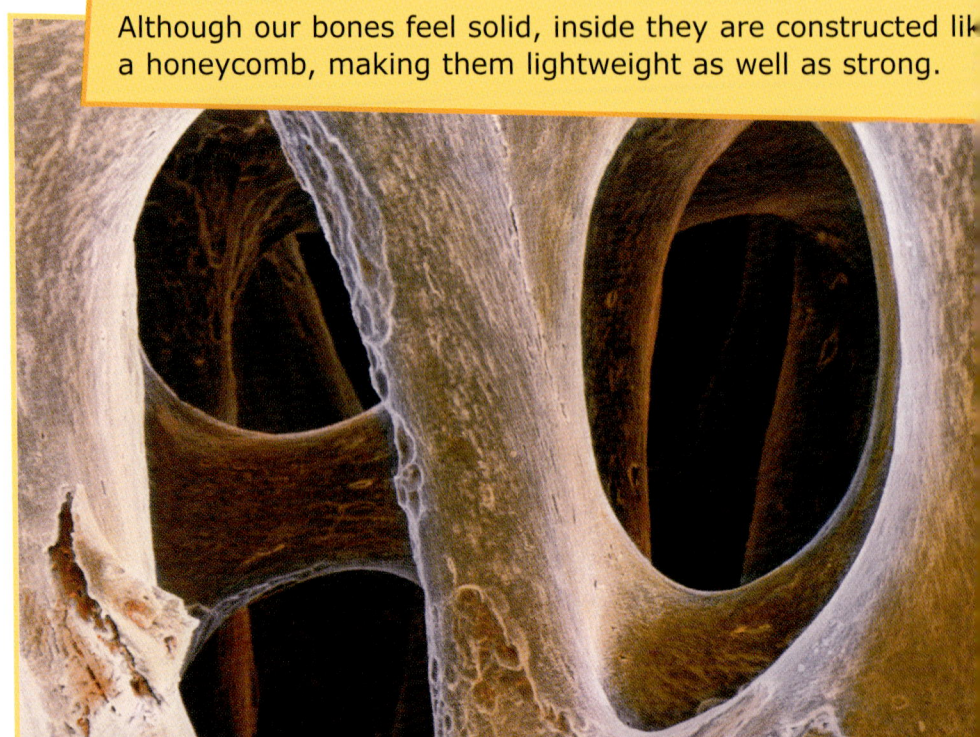

Although our bones feel solid, inside they are constructed like a honeycomb, making them lightweight as well as strong.

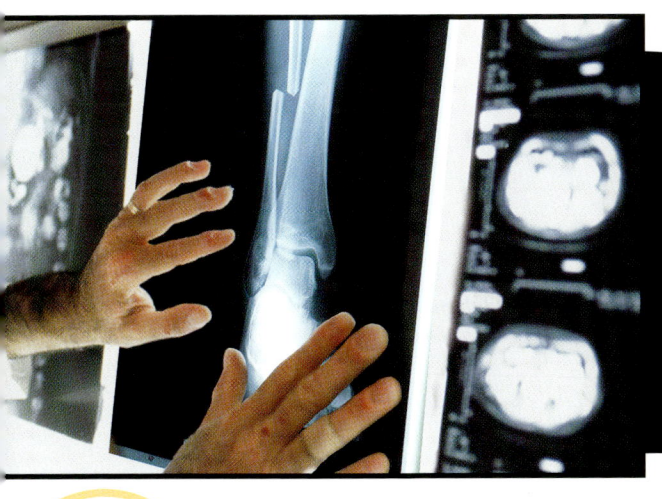

Bones can be seen clearly on X-rays. Broken bones actually heal themselves. A plaster cast, splint or other support just holds the bone in the right position while it mends.

IN FOCUS

Osteoporosis is a disease that can make older people's bones weak and brittle. Often the way people find out that they have osteoporosis is by breaking or fracturing a bone. Getting enough calcium and plenty of exercise are important ways to help prevent osteoporosis.

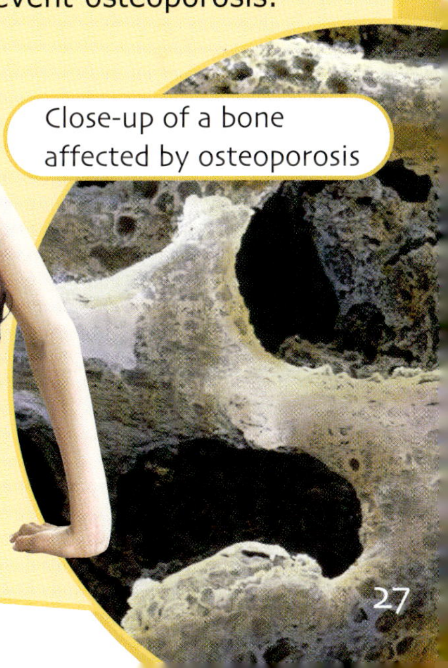

Close-up of a bone affected by osteoporosis

Spare Parts

For centuries people have used the technology and materials available to make spare parts for the body. Eyes were usually made of glass. False teeth have been made of many different materials, including wood, ivory and gold. Artificial arms and legs were made of wood or metal. These were sometimes rigid, or they were flexible with hinges and levers.

Today most parts of the body can be replaced by **prostheses**. Some prostheses do the actual job of the missing body parts, while others such as false eyes are **cosmetic**.

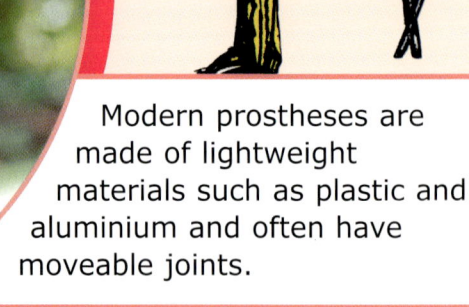

Modern prostheses are made of lightweight materials such as plastic and aluminium and often have moveable joints.

When a person's kidneys are diseased, a renal (kidney) dialysis machine is used to do the job of the kidneys—filtering and cleaning blood. Tubes carry the patient's blood to the machine and back again.

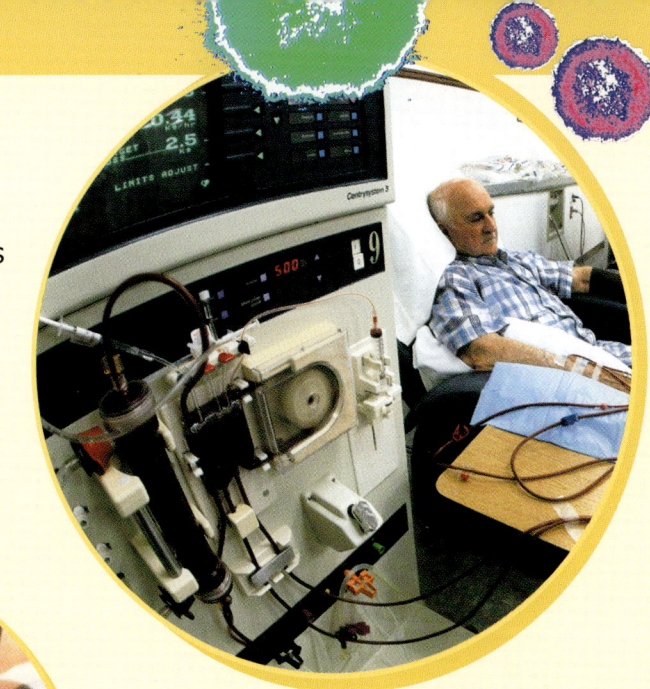

The use of artificial skin allows the real skin underneath to heal naturally.

IN FOCUS

Today many damaged or diseased organs and limbs can be replaced with real parts provided by organ donors. The first transplant was of a part of the eye called the cornea in 1905. The first heart transplant was performed in 1967.

This heart is ready for transplantation.

Glossary

anatomy – the study of human or animal body structures

blood platelet – a small flat cell fragment found in large numbers in the blood. It assists the clotting of blood in wounds.

cadaver – a dead body

circulatory system – the network of heart and blood vessels that moves blood around the body

conscious – aware of what's happening and able to think and reason

cosmetic – something that changes a person's looks

diagnosis – the identification of a patient's disease made after studying the symptoms

dominant – a characteristic that appears even when inherited from only one parent

hallucinate – to see things that aren't there

insomnia – the inability to fall asleep or get back to sleep

neuron – a nerve cell

physiology – the study of how living things function

prosthesis – a substitute for a natural body part that has not developed properly or has been damaged by injury or disease. The plural of prosthesis is prostheses.

recessive – a characteristic that will not appear unless inherited from both parents

skeletal – having to do with the skeleton

subconscious – a part of our mind that influences actions and feelings without our knowing

trait – a characteristic such as hair or eye colour

Index

allergies	18–19, 22
anatomy	5–6
artificial body parts	28–29
asthma	22
blood	5, 18, 20–22, 29
bones	20–21, 24–27
brain	12–17
breathing	22–23
cells	6–8, 12–13, 18–22, 24–26
DNA	8–9
genes	8–11
immune system	18–19
lungs	20–23
muscles	7, 12–13, 16, 24–26
nerves	7, 12–13
osteoporosis	27
Parkinson disease	14
physiology	5–6
rheumatoid arthritis	19
skin	8, 13, 19, 29
sleep	16–17
spinal cord	12–13
X-rays	6–7, 27

Research Starters

1 Do you remember your dreams? Keep a dream journal by your bed and write down your dreams as soon as you wake up every morning for two weeks. Record how many dreams you remember and at what times of the night you think they occurred. Then make a graph of the data.

2 How does blood donation benefit society? Find out where the blood donation centre is in your area and how the blood is used. Then ask someone you know who has donated blood about why they decided to donate.

3 Which aspects of your looks and your personality do you share with other members of your family? Make lists of the similar and the different characteristics that you and the others have. Which ones do you think are due to natural inheritance and which to environment or experiences?

4 Imagine you lost a limb such as an arm or a leg. How would it affect your life? Research the ways in which modern technology could help you continue to enjoy the same activities you do today.